What Was D-Day?

by Patricia Brennan Demuth

illustrated by David Grayson Kenyon

Penguin Workshop

For all the brave who fight for
freedom and peace—PBD

PENGUIN WORKSHOP
An Imprint of Penguin Random House LLC, New York

Text copyright © 2015 by Patricia Brennan.
Illustrations copyright © 2015 by Penguin Random House LLC. All rights reserved. Published
by Penguin Workshop, an imprint of Penguin Random House LLC, New York. PENGUIN
and PENGUIN WORKSHOP are trademarks of Penguin Books Ltd. WHO HQ & Design
is a registered trademark of Penguin Random House LLC. Printed in the USA.

Visit us online at www.penguinrandomhouse.com.

Library of Congress Control Number: 2015939764

ISBN 9780448484075   20 19

Contents

What Was D-Day?

June 6, 1944

In the dark hours before dawn, a giant war fleet was sailing across the English Channel to France. There were over 5,000 ships and boats of all shapes and sizes. More than 155,000 soldiers were on board—mostly American, British, and Canadian. They were called the Allies. *Allies* means friends joined together in a cause.

Another huge Allied force had just flown over the channel to France, filling 11,000 airplanes. All of these soldiers, on boats and in planes, were risking their lives to invade Europe and end World War II.

The Second World War had been raging for five years. It had started in 1939 when Adolf Hitler, the leader of Nazi (NAHT-see) Germany, invaded Poland. Now more than thirty nations were part of the war. The Germans had overtaken nearly all of mainland Europe. And World War II had become the bloodiest war that ever was.

The Allies were fighting Hitler. But so far, they had almost no troops on the ground in Europe—let alone in Germany itself. There was only one way the Allies could defeat Nazi Germany and free Europe. They had to fight—and beat—Hitler on his home ground.

But how?

First the Allies had to land a huge army on the coast of France—plus tanks, trucks, and supplies. Then they had to fight their way inland for 700 miles to reach Berlin, the capital of Germany.

For nearly two years, the Allies planned the great invasion. Millions of people worked on it. Engineers invented new war machines. Factory workers produced new planes and tanks. Spies fed Hitler false reports. And nearly two million Allied soldiers trained hard in Britain.

Yet the whole invasion could fall apart. The Germans had built a wall of steel and concrete defenses up and down the coast. Could the first waves of Allied soldiers break through and gain control of the beaches and exit roads? That was the only way the rest of the troops could land.

If the D-Day soldiers failed, all would be lost. There was no backup plan. The Allies had thrown everything they had into this one.

"D-Day" is a code word for the day of any major military attack. But when people talk about "D-Day" now, they mean June 6, 1944. D-Day was a turning point in history—it was the beginning of the end of World War II.

CHAPTER 1
The World at War

Germany was one of the countries defeated in World War I. That war killed nearly ten million soldiers between 1914 and 1918. After Germany surrendered, its cities lay in ruins and its economy was in shreds. There were hardly any jobs. People were starving.

Then in 1933, Adolf Hitler, the leader of the Nazi party, rose to power. He stamped out democracy, making himself the dictator of Germany. Freedom disappeared. Hitler named certain groups enemies, especially the Jews.

The Holocaust

Adolf Hitler, the Nazi leader of Germany, hated the Jewish people. His answer for solving Germany's problems was to get rid of all Jews. During the war, Hitler had eleven million people killed, including six million Jews. No one really understands what made Hitler commit such evil acts. The name given to the killing of these innocents is the *Holocaust*.

Hitler built up a powerful army with millions of well-trained soldiers. Their weapons were the best in the world. Then he set plans to conquer all of Europe . . . and beyond.

Without warning, in September 1939, Germany invaded Poland. First, bomber planes blasted Polish railroads, airfields, and telegraph lines. Then more than a million German ground troops plowed into Poland with tanks and heavy arms. This kind of attack—bombing followed by a crush of tanks—is called *lightning war*. The German word is *blitzkrieg*, or *blitz* for short.

England and France immediately declared war on Germany. World War II had begun.

England and France were no match for the powerful Hitler. After Poland fell, German troops crashed through Denmark, Norway, Belgium, Luxembourg, and the Netherlands. In June 1940, France itself fell to the Germans. The free world was in shock.

On the other side of the world, Japan was overtaking lands in Asia and the Pacific. Japan signed an agreement with Germany in September 1940. Along with Italy, the three countries were called the Axis powers.

World War II Leaders

World War II was fought between groups of nations known as the Axis and the Allies. The major Axis leaders were Adolf Hitler (Germany), Benito Mussolini (Italy), and Hideki Tojo (Japan).

Italy	**Germany**	**Japan**
Benito Mussolini	Adolf Hitler	Hideki Tojo

Shown below are the leaders of the major Allied powers, known as the "Big Three":

Great Britain	**United States**	**Soviet Union**
Prime Minister	President	Joseph Stalin
Winston Churchill	Franklin D. Roosevelt	

Meanwhile in Europe, British troops stood alone against Hitler. The United States shipped Britain arms, tanks, and planes. But for now, the United States did not send troops. More than 115,000 American soldiers had been killed in World War I. The country did not want to fight another war overseas.

Then on December 7, 1941, the Japanese led a surprise air attack against American forces at Pearl Harbor in Hawaii. More than two thousand American troops died. The next day, US President Franklin Roosevelt declared war against Japan and its allies, including Germany.

From then on, the United States played a key role in World War II. American men enlisted in huge numbers. The US military grew from 334,000 men at the beginning of the war to a force of twelve million.

Overnight, the nation turned itself into a war factory. Thousands of warplanes, battleships, and arms were churned out and shipped overseas. In 1939, America made fewer than a thousand military planes a year. By the end of 1943, it produced eight thousand per *month*.

Yet Hitler and the Axis powers seemed unstoppable. Hitler overran almost all of Europe. His troops marched east into the Soviet Union. Japan seized countries in Southeast Asia and the Pacific. Italy was winning battles in North Africa. At the beginning of 1942, news from the Allied war front was grim.

Rescue at Dunkirk

British troops could not stand up to Nazi Germany alone after France fell. The Germans defeated them in battle after battle, pushing them back toward the west coast of Europe. By June 1940, 338,000 troops, including French, were trapped in a narrow strip of coastline at Dunkirk, France. In a daring rescue, hundreds of private boats carried them back to England. The quick getaway forced Britain to leave behind thousands of guns and more than 100,000 vehicles.

Then slowly, one hard battle at a time, the Allies began to gain ground. Japan's advance was halted at a small island in the Pacific called Midway. The Soviets stopped Hitler's advance in Russia. Allied troops forced Italy out of Africa. The Italians then overthrew their dictator, Mussolini, and signed a truce with the Allies.

There was a surge of hope. Allied leaders began planning a strategy for ending the terrible war.

CHAPTER 2
A Bold Plan

The Atlantic Ocean borders mainland Europe on the west. During the war, Hitler knew this coastline was open to attack. So in 1942, he ordered a line of defenses built on the coast. He called it the Atlantic Wall. It stretched for

2,400 miles along the shoreline. If there was an invasion, Hitler planned to end it on the first day.

Two hundred fifty thousand workers, including French prisoners, were forced to build the defenses. They planted six million mines. Each was set to explode as soon as an Allied soldier stepped on it. They lined the beaches with thick nets of barbed wire. And they planted steel spikes and great logs in the sand to gash the bottoms of boats at high tide.

Concrete bunkers and forts of all sizes were built behind the beaches. A network of trenches linked them together. Almost a million tons of concrete was poured into the bunkers in one month alone. Gun holes pointed straight at the coast. Hitler aimed to wipe out enemy soldiers the minute they hit the beaches.

While the Germans built the Atlantic Wall, the Allies made plans to bust through it—on D-Day. Early in 1942, President Roosevelt and Prime Minister Churchill decided to invade in the spring of 1944. That gave them about a year and a half to prepare the attack and train the troops.

The next question was *where* to land. The shortest, easiest route was to Calais, France. It was just twenty miles from Dover, England. But the Germans would expect the Allies to land there. The invasion had to take the Germans by surprise. So the Allies decided to land at the unlikely spot of Normandy, France—a hundred miles away.

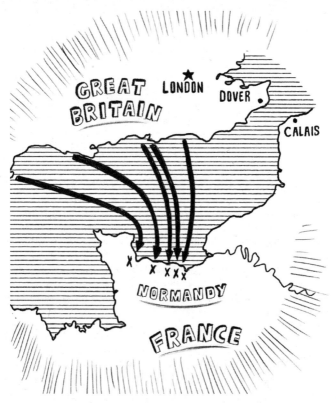

Timing was tricky. The Allies wanted troops to parachute in at night to take the Germans by surprise. The moon had to be full. Otherwise paratroopers couldn't see well enough in the dark. The boats would land at dawn after stealing across the channel under cover of darkness. The tide had to be low because German obstacles on the coast would tear boats apart at high tide.

Five Beaches at Normandy

On D-Day, the Allies attacked five major beaches that stretched for sixty miles down the coast of Normandy, France. Every beach was a separate battleground with its own battle plan and attack forces. The beaches were all given code names. The plan called for British troops to land at Sword and Gold, Canadian troops at Juno, and American troops at Omaha and Utah.

An American general was put in charge of the invasion. His name was Dwight D. Eisenhower—"Ike" for short. Ike was a quiet man with a big grin. At West Point he had been known for playing pranks. Later, however, Ike stood out as a master planner and organizer. He also inspired other soldiers. "He merely has to smile at you, and you trust him at once," said a British general named Bernard Montgomery.

Ike went over the plans for D-Day in late 1943. There wasn't enough "wallop," he said. He wanted more of everything—more soldiers, guns, tanks, and planes. Under his orders, the United States began shipping planes, tanks, arms, boats, ships, jeeps, and trucks to England. By D-Day,

Americans had given five million tons of supplies and equipment.

Ike also sent more than a million more American soldiers to Britain. They joined all the other Allied troops training there for the great invasion. By D-Day, there were 1.7 million Americans, a million British and Canadians, and about three hundred thousand men from other countries in Europe.

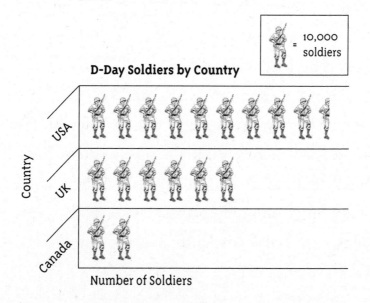

D-Day Soldiers by Country

= 10,000 soldiers

Country

USA

UK

Canada

Number of Soldiers

Training was hard and intense. Paratroopers practiced jumping from planes and marching for three days straight. Soldiers practiced firing weapons, climbing cliffs, and crawling under barbed wire while live fire whizzed overhead.

Yet not one soldier knew where or when he would fight. D-Day was kept top secret.

CHAPTER 3
Fooling Hitler

Hitler knew that the Allies were planning to invade Western Europe. However, he didn't know where or when. To keep Hitler in the dark, the Allies used spies, lies, and clever tricks. Special teams were formed, including engineers, double agents, and moviemakers.

To fake out the Germans, the Allies set up a big army base in Dover, England. Dover was right across from Calais, France. The base looked real—but it was phony. German spy planes flying overhead saw hundreds of tanks that seemed made of steel. But really, they were made of rubber, blown up like giant balloons!

Sounds of clanking tanks blared from recordings. Even the tire tracks that led away from the tanks were faked.

It also looked as if trucks, jeeps, planes, and ships filled the base. They were actually made out of painted canvas, stretched over wooden frames. The pretend army was a genius mix of Hollywood and high tech.

CLANG CLANG CLANG CLANG CLANG CLANG

US General George Patton was chosen to "lead" the make-believe army at Dover. Patton was the Allies' most famous general—just the man Hitler expected to head a real attack. The Allies had newspapers run stories with photos of Patton visiting his bogus troops. Radio airwaves broadcast false news about plans set for Calais. German spies picked up the radio messages and relayed them to Hitler.

The bluff worked. Hitler sent 200,000 of his best soldiers to Calais to fight an invasion that never came. He didn't leave the Normandy beaches unguarded. But on D-Day when the Allies landed there, all the Calais troops were two hundred miles away from where the real fighting took place!

Many of Hitler's spies had actually become double agents. They had landed in England by parachute, rubber boats, and submarines. Once there, however, most of the spies were captured. They ended up working for the Allies while still pretending to be on Hitler's side! The spies fed Hitler a steady stream of false information. It was a dangerous setup. If one double agent was found out, Hitler would suspect the whole scheme. But he never did.

Double Trouble

The Allies' cleverest double agent went by the name Garbo. (His real name was Juan Pujol Garcia.) He invented a group of thirty-six spies that fed Hitler secret reports from all over England. Garbo and his "spies" gave Hitler pieces of real information to gain his trust. Then the Nazis were fed lies. Hitler found the reports so believable that he awarded Garbo his highest medal of honor! On D-Day itself, Garbo convinced Hitler that the attack was not the real invasion. "You have to believe me," he said. And Hitler did.

A network of spies also worked in France. Tens of thousands of French men and women were in the French Resistance. These daring citizens did whatever they could to undermine the Nazis: they rescued stranded airmen, forged papers, and reported on the up-to-date comings and goings of German troops. French artists drew maps of Normandy landmarks to prepare Allied soldiers for D-Day.

How did the French slip messages into England? One way was by using carrier pigeons! The birds flew eight hours round-trip across the English Channel with messages attached to their claws!

The tricks played by the Allies continued right up to the attack. Early on D-Day morning, planes dropped hundreds of "paratroopers" far from the real battle sites. Although dressed in helmets and uniforms, the paratroopers were dummies. Bombs attached to the dummies burst into flames upon landing. Some real troopers landed near the dummies and added to the effects of a major battle. They lit flares and

blared sounds of gunfire over loudspeakers. They sent out chemicals that smelled like exploding shells. German troops fell for it. Hundreds of soldiers raced to the phony attack site—in the opposite direction of the real one!

The Allies' false reports, fake armies, and misleading radio signals saved countless lives on D-Day—and afterward.

During an interview after the war, Ike grinned and said, "By God, we really fooled 'em, didn't we?"

CHAPTER 4
Countdown to D-Day

D-Day was scheduled for June 5, 1944 at first. As the date grew nearer, Allied fighter pilots flew missions over Europe. They were able to shoot

down 1,300 German planes. This helped to prevent a German air attack on D-Day. Bombers also exploded bridges and railroads all over France. Once the invasion began, the enemy would have trouble sending backup troops to Normandy. The Allies left some travel routes open so troops could push into Germany after D-Day.

In early May, nearly two million soldiers crowded into harbors in the south of England. Boats and planes waited to carry them into battle. "All Southern England was one vast military camp," said General Eisenhower. It took 4,500 cooks just to make their meals. People joked that the tip of the island would sink under the soldiers' weight.

Now, for the first time, soldiers opened and read their orders. They pored over huge war maps that rolled up like rugs. Separately, the units rehearsed their individual attack plans. And each soldier practiced using the kind of weapon he was assigned.

By June 3, troops piled into waiting ships set to land at Normandy on the fifth. All systems were go. Then a terrible storm brought everything to a screeching halt. Weather reports said the storm would last for days.

Southwick House, Eisenhower's headquarters in England

Because of the weather, Nazi General Erwin Rommel left Normandy to visit his wife in Germany. He was sure the bad storm would prevent Allies from attacking. In England, Ike postponed the invasion for twenty-four hours.

In the early hours of June 5, General Eisenhower met with his high command at a manor in southern England. Wind rattled the windows and rain pelted the glass.

The commanders listened to the latest weather report. A slight break in the weather was possible for June 6.

Should they risk making a full-scale attack now—or wait? If they didn't attack now, they'd have to wait a whole month for another full moon.

Ike polled the officers around the table. Opinions were mixed. The final decision, however, was Eisenhower's alone. Ike was under great pressure. Going out in the storm risked the lives of his soldiers and the success of the attack. On the other hand, delay meant that the Germans might discover the plan. That put lives at risk, too.

Finally, just after 4:00 a.m., Ike gave the command: "Okay, let's go."

That night, Eisenhower visited a division of paratroopers (soldiers who parachute into battle). These were the soldiers who would first see action on D-Day. Ike mingled among them, giving a thumbs-up and telling them not to worry. "I've done all I can," Ike told the men. "Now it is up to you." Many troopers had blackened their faces so the enemy couldn't spot them in the dark. Some had shaved their heads like Mohawk warriors.

Loaded With Gear

Paratroopers had enough gear to survive on their own for several days in case a bad landing separated them from their units. Here are some of the things they carried:

- parachute on his back
- extra chute on his chest
- rifle and bullets
- hand grenades
- smoke grenades
- antitank mines
- steel helmet
- water canteen
- wrist compass
- spoon
- French money

- food

- gas mask

- life jacket

- three knives

- jump boots

- padded drop bag

- jump jacket and pants

- bayonet

- trench knife

- first-aid kit

- raincoat

The paratroopers were loaded with up to two hundred pounds of gear. They had to be ready to survive on their own if necessary. One small private looked like "more equipment than soldier," Ike said. The soldier exchanged salutes with his commander. Then he turned toward France and said, "Look out, Hitler, here we come!"

Finally, the paratroopers boarded their planes and soared into the sky. Ike watched them head into the dark unknown. There was nothing Ike could do now but wait for radio reports from the field.

"Well, it's on," Ike said. "No one can stop it now." His eyes were wet with tears.

CHAPTER 5
Dropping into Darkness

Just after midnight on June 6, 1944, the largest air fleet in history began winging its way across the English Channel. More than eight hundred planes lifted off from air bases scattered around England. In the air, the planes formed perfect long lines. About 20,000 paratroopers were on board. They were going to parachute into enemy territory in the dark!

Usually the paratroopers joked around with one another. Many had become good friends after training hard together for nearly two years. But that night, "the men sat quietly, deep in their own thoughts," said General Matthew B. Ridgway.

No doubt, they were thinking ahead to their dangerous goal. They had to take control of the important bridges and roads that led away from the beaches. These routes were the only way the

Allies could move big numbers of troops inland—and right now they were heavily guarded by Germans. The Allies had already destroyed other major bridges and roads, so these routes were key.

The airplanes neared Normandy about 1:30 a.m. Suddenly, planes started rocking wildly and veered off course. The air blazed with tracer bullets fired from German guns on the ground. Blue, green, and yellow streaks lit up the sky like fireworks.

Soldiers lurched inside as their planes took hits. The shells sounded "like someone threw a keg of nails against the side of the airplane," said Sergeant Dan Furlong.

Airplanes turned into death traps. Pilots opened hatch doors and flashed the green light— the signal for paratroopers to jump. According to the plan, it was much too soon. The locations where they were supposed to land were still far away! And yet it was safer to jump than to stay aboard the aircraft. "The green light popped on

and, 'Go Geronimo,' we all jumped," said trooper Carl Cartledge. "I've never been so glad to get out of an airplane in my life!"

Chaos filled the sky. Thousands of planes were swerving off course, trying not to collide. Enemy machine fire caught troopers in the air. Burning aircraft exploded and plunged to earth. Troopers landed all over—in fields, trees, and barns. Hardly any ended up at the correct spots.

Some troopers hit the ground at high speeds. They stayed black-and-blue for days. Landing in water was even worse. Paratroopers plunged into fields that the Germans had flooded in order to block the advance of Allied troops. Fighting for their lives, soldiers struggled to break free from heavy gear and tangled chutes. Hundreds drowned.

Seventeen-year-old Ken Russell dangled from the roof of a village church! Ken had lied about his age in order to join the army. In Normandy, he managed to free himself and jump twenty feet to the ground. Then he went into combat on his own against Germans firing at Allied planes. Later, he met up with more paratroopers to attack German gun sites.

Thousands of other troopers also landed alone and lost in the dark. The men were supposed to link up with their units as soon as they were on the ground. On D-Day, however, for most, this never happened. Instead, they joined up with men they'd never seen before. Or they fought alone. They fought Germans wherever they found them, inventing attack plans on the spot.

Lieutenant Richard "Dick" Winters, a paratrooper from a team called Easy Company, landed in the middle of nowhere without a gun. His rifle had been whipped away in the air. Winters unstrapped the knife from his ankle and set out to find the thirty-two men in his troop.

Suddenly figures loomed in the darkness ahead. Were they friend or foe? Winters snapped his "cricket." It was a tiny clicker that troopers used to identify each other at night. He heard two clicks back: *click-clack, click-clack*. Good! That meant Allied troops. Luckily, Winters had found five men from his own troop, Easy Company.

Eventually, thirteen men of Easy Company linked up on D-Day. Their commander was missing. (He died when his plane exploded.) So Winters became their leader. The small force captured four big enemy cannons that were tearing up Utah Beach—even though the Germans guarding the tanks outnumbered them four to one.

The brave efforts of paratroopers met with other successes. German soldiers couldn't make sense of the scattered attack "pattern," and they failed to counterattack. Most important, the paratroopers seized key exit bridges and roads.

However, by the end of D-Day, the paratroopers had suffered a terrible toll. About one out of five was killed, wounded, or taken prisoner. As a result, the US military never had troops parachute in at night again.

Silent Wings

Not all paratroopers flew in on planes. Hundreds of gliders made of plywood also carried paratroopers. Since they had no engines, the gliders were pulled across the channel by planes. The towrope was released a couple of hundred yards from the landing site. From there, glider pilots steered the drifting planes the rest of the way to the ground.

Just after midnight on June 6, gliders landed only feet away from two major bridges over the Caen Canal and Orne river. Stunned German guards soon surrendered the bridges, giving the Allies their first victory on D-Day.

CHAPTER 6
Stormy Seas

In the dark hours before dawn on June 6, 1944, 5,000 vessels of all shapes and sizes crammed the waters of the English Channel. It was the largest invasion by sea of all time. The fleet ranged from giant ships carrying 5,000 tons of cargo to small landing boats. The ships and boats seemed to be "in a mass so solid one could have walked from shore to shore."

More than 155,000 young soldiers filled the passenger ships. Their average age was only twenty-two. Two out of every ten had never even been in a battle before. The ships carried 20,000 tons of ammunition—all for the first day alone.

Germans had loaded the channel with floating mines. The bombs were set to explode when a

ship passed over them. But the fleet crossed safely, thanks to tiny boats called *minesweepers* that cleared the waters earlier.

Minesweeper

Twelve miles from shore, the ships stopped. Soldiers clambered down ropes into small landing boats that would carry them the rest of the way to Normandy. There were no seats inside. Men stood, squatted, or sat wherever they could.

In the boats were units of soldiers who had trained together and rehearsed battle plans. Each

unit included about thirty men. Every soldier had
become an expert at using a certain weapon. There
were machine gunners and riflemen. There were
soldiers with *bazookas*—guns that fired exploding
rockets. Some had flamethrowers, weapons that
burst burning gasoline. Wire cutters had tools for
slashing barbed-wire traps. Mortar teams fired
long-range exploding shells. Each troop was a
small army itself.

Yet all the power on the boats couldn't stop the terrible problems from the storm. Even getting to shore was hard. Trouble started as soon as the troops transferred to the small wooden boats. Cold, stormy seawater poured over the rims. Soaked soldiers had to use their helmets to bail out water. The choppy swells made many men seasick. A few hours earlier, the navy had treated the troops to a hearty breakfast: steak, eggs, pork chops, ice cream, beans, and bacon. Now full stomachs made the soldiers sicker than ever.

"It was a terrible ride to the beach," recalled squad leader Bob Slaughter in the PBS film *D-Day Remembered*. "A tremendous tsunami swamped our boat, and the water would come over the side and just soak us and make our seasickness worse."

Meanwhile, up ahead at the beaches, the stormy weather was causing problems for over four hundred Allied bomber planes. They were heading into Normandy to bomb German gun posts before the ground troops came ashore. Unfortunately, thick storm clouds hid targets on the ground. Pilots had to steer by radar, which was new at the time. They feared dropping their bombs too early and destroying Allied ships in the channel! Pilots were ordered to hold their bombs until they knew for sure they were past the beaches.

The bombing raids relied on exact timing. Even a thirty-second delay meant bombs would miss their targets by over a mile. That's exactly what happened at Omaha Beach on D-Day. By the time Allied planes dropped their 13,000 bombs, they were well past the beaches. Most of the bombs landed in farm fields or cow pastures. Not one hit its target!

The storm also ruined another D-Day plan. Heavy armed tanks were supposed to land on the beaches just ahead of the soldiers. The huge cannons would provide fire cover as the soldiers swept the beaches. Weighing several tons, the cannons were much too big for the small landing boats to carry. So the Allies had invented "swimming tanks" that could plow through the water under their own power. High canvas sides made the tanks look like huge covered wagons rising out of the sea.

The swimming tanks had aced test runs, but they weren't built for heavy seas. Six-foot waves smashed over their sides as they approached Omaha Beach on D-Day. Twenty-seven tanks heading to Omaha sank to the bottom of the Channel. Three more became dead in the water. Only two made it to shore, but too late to help.

That meant soldiers had to fight across the beach on their own with no cover at all.

CHAPTER 7
Bloody Omaha

At 6:30 a.m., dawn on D-Day, the small landing boats began arriving at Normandy. At last, the full-scale attack of the beaches was at hand.

Most soldiers arrived feeling cold, wet, and sick. Despite all their training, they were about to face overwhelming firepower from the Germans.

The landing at Utah Beach went like clockwork. This was thanks mostly to the paratroopers who had disarmed the big German guns the night before.

At Gold, Juno, and Sword beaches, soldiers had to overcome greater enemy fire. And at Omaha, American troops faced the worst conditions of all. The terrible battle fought there became known as "Bloody Omaha."

Omaha was a key beach because it lay at the center of Normandy. It stretched for six miles between Utah and Gold. Omaha was also the most difficult beach to invade, so the Allies sent twice the number of troops there. Unlike the other beaches, Omaha was backed by a wall of cliffs a hundred feet high. Over a thousand Germans were in bunkers on top. They fired down from their perches, as if from a rooftop.

The boats stopped a few hundred yards from shore, and landing ramps were lowered. Soldiers needed to wade in the rest of the way. Germans let loose with a fury of firepower. Bullets ripped at the sides of boats, capsizing many. One shell hit a boat filled with explosives, blowing it sky-high. All men on board were killed instantly.

Germans aimed their machine guns straight at the exit ramps of the small boats. Bullets hit the Allied soldiers the second they stepped onto the ramp. Private First Class Robert "Bob" Sales recalled those terrible first moments at Omaha: "The ramp went down and [our captain] was the first man off, and they just riddled him." Sales was the only survivor of the more than thirty men in his boat. "We were cut to pieces," he said.

Hitler's Zipper

Nazi soldiers blasted the landing boats with MG-42s. They were the fastest machine guns in the world at that time, double the speed of the American Browning. The guns fired at 2,000 miles per hour, 125 bullets every second. The rapid sound of its gunfire earned it the name "Hitler's zipper."

Men landed in water over their heads. Weighted down by gear and weak from seasickness, they struggled underwater for their lives. "I really panicked," said Private First Class Sales. He shed his radio, gun, and jacket just in time to rise back to the surface.

Soldiers who survived the landing tried to reach shore. "We had about five hundred yards of water to cross," Lieutenant Colonel Alfred F. Birra later wrote in a letter home. "We couldn't run because the water was too deep. We couldn't crouch. We couldn't do anything except just what we did." They pushed forward, bullets whizzing overhead. The surf turned red with the blood of the wounded and dying.

Near the coastline, men tried to hide behind some of the steel defenses set up by the Germans. It was no use against the enemy's long-range weapons. "All I could see was chaos, catastrophe," Chuck Hurlbut, combat engineer, recalled. "Boats burning, smoking, dead men all along the water's edge . . ."

Soldiers staggered onto the beach, but dry land offered little relief. The "killing zone" lay ahead—one thousand feet of open, dangerous beach. Before soldiers could reach the cliffs, they

had to get past jagged steel beams, sharp barbed wire, and seventeen thousand buried mines.

An hour after landing, the battle at Omaha was an all-out disaster. All the fire had come from enemy guns. The Allies had barely fired a shot. Soldiers fought just to save their lives.

D-Day was not going according to plan.

CHAPTER 8
Leaders Step Up

An hour into the invasion, things seemed hopeless for the Allies at Omaha. The battle was at a complete standstill. Wounded and dead filled the beach. Survivors huddled in groups wherever they could escape enemy fire. Many of them were wounded and without weapons. All were weak and exhausted.

How had it come to this? "We were a proud outfit. We were well-trained, well-disciplined, and believed that nobody could defeat us," said Hal Baumgarten. "There were these guys . . . stacked up . . . dead. And, of course, the blood was all over the place. It was horrible."

Deadly Fire

Mortar is a portable cannon that fires exploding shells. The mortar fire hitting the Normandy beaches killed Allied troops in two ways. Shrapnel—bits of hot metal—flew out from the explosions at 7,000 miles per hour. It's "like a thousand different bullets going everyplace at the same time," explained Marine Sergeant. William Bodette. The mortar also released blasts of air pushing outward at superhigh speeds. One such blast wounded Harold "Hal" Baumgarten on Omaha Beach. It "felt like somebody hit me with a baseball bat," he reported in *Surviving D-Day.*

Then, just when defeat seemed certain, leaders rose up among the men. Individual soldiers, acting on their own at separate spots, stepped forward and got the attack moving again.

At 7:30 a.m., First Lieutenant William Moody was hiding at the bottom of the cliffs with about twenty-five other guys. They huddled inside shallow sea caves dug out by the water. For the moment, they were safely out of range of the German gunners firing from the cliffs overhead.

Moody decided to do something—*anything* but sit and wait. How could he move his men up the cliff and fight back? The rock was much too steep to climb where they were. Moody motioned for two soldiers to follow him. Soon they were hiking along the base of the cliffs in search of a better spot to climb. A few hundred yards away, they discovered a crack that ran from the top of the cliff to the bottom.

Moody jabbed his bayonet into the cliff's face and pulled himself up a few feet. Doing it again, he pulled up a few feet more. The two soldiers behind him followed suit. Somehow the three men reached the top without setting off land mines.

Survivor at Omaha

Among the first soldiers to arrive at Omaha was Private Hal Baumgarten, just nineteen years old. He was one of two men on his landing boat to survive. The others were killed or wounded when they stepped into the opening of the exit ramp. Hal's life was saved when he tripped and fell into the water. But enemy fire would hit Hal five times during the next thirty-two hours! Half of his cheek was ripped off by a mortar blast. Still, Hal kept moving forward. After the war, he wrote his memories of that terrible battle. Hal believed his life had been spared so that he could "be the spokesman for those true heroes who perished [on D-Day]."

At the top, they pounded in stakes and let down rope ladders to the ground. Moody ran along the cliff to the place directly above where the soldiers waited in caves. The men stared up at the impossible: Lieutenant Moody had somehow made it to the top!

The soldiers took off running in the direction to which Moody pointed until they found the hanging ladders. Leaning far back on the rope pulls, the soldiers monkey-walked their way up the rock.

Though a German bullet killed Moody later that day, he is remembered as a D-Day hero: the man to lead the first unit on Omaha to reach high ground.

Though Moody's group had made it uphill, hundreds of other soldiers at Omaha were still stuck on the beach. Many of them were huddling along a seawall that ran the length of the beach, about two-thirds of the way to the bluffs. The seawall, which stood about five feet high, was the only place to hide on the open beach. Dazed and confused, the soldiers were a jumbled mix of units. Most of their leaders, usually the first ones off the boats, were missing or dead.

The tide was quickly creeping in and covering

the shore. By 9:30 a.m., seawater already covered most of Omaha Beach. That left the men pinned in on two sides! Ahead of them were German gunners. Behind them, the rising tide.

General Norman "Dutch" Cota was watching the men through binoculars from a boat offshore. At fifty-one, Cota was the oldest soldier at Omaha. As a general, he was supposed to stay on the ship and radio in commands. But this was crisis time.

Dutch tossed out the rules, grabbed a gun, and waded to shore. The men stuck at the seawall suddenly looked out to see this stocky man running across the beach, smoking a cigar! "He was fearless," a soldier recalled.

At the seawall, Cota inspired the men into action. He spoke these now-famous words: "Gentlemen, we are being killed on the beaches. Let us go inland and be killed." Soon the soldiers were picking up weapons on the beach, finding helmets, and cleaning the sand from their rifles.

A tangled mass of spiky barbed wire, planted by the enemy, blocked the way forward. The men blasted a hole through the sharp wire with a torpedo and dynamite, then dashed for the bluffs. A rain of German bullets killed many, but Cota led the rest up the bluff.

Finally, they could meet the enemy face-to-face.

CHAPTER 9
Mission Accomplished!

Cota and his troops had cut through enemy lines! The news reached a dozen destroyers anchored offshore at Omaha. The job of the destroyers was to protect the troop ships waiting offshore. But fresh orders sent them full speed ahead to the beach. Near the shoreline, the huge ships turned broadside and unleashed firepower from their cannons.

Every minute, more Allied troops were storming up the cliff. Battles atop the cliffs now raged. Firing flamethrowers and hurling grenades, the Allies flushed the enemy out of bunkers and trenches. German soldiers were too busy defending themselves to fire on the beaches.

By 1:30 p.m., US troops were on their way to controlling Omaha Beach. About an hour before, Hitler had received word that "the invasion [at Normandy] had been completely smashed." The report was very wrong.

Time and again, Allied troops reached their limits—and pushed beyond. Wounded soldiers kept on fighting. Officers led squads even as they died. "I asked [the troops] to die for freedom and they were ready to do it," General Eisenhower said later, "and that's why they are heroes."

When night closed, victory belonged to the Allies. The mission of D-Day was accomplished! The Allies had taken all five beaches and advanced up to ten miles inland. They were freeing French towns, taking German prisoners, and tearing down Nazi flags.

The Germans found it hard to fight back. Bombing had destroyed many of their key roads and train tracks, forcing backup troops on long detours. Plus, Hitler still thought the Normandy invasion was a setup. So he delayed moving troops, which were farther north, where he expected the "real" attack.

As darkness fell on D-Day, relief and pride filled the survivors. "The first night in France I spent in a ditch beside a hedgerow wrapped in a damp [tent piece] and thoroughly exhausted. But I felt elated," said Sergeant John Ellery. "No matter what had happened, I had made it off the beach and reached the high ground."

"I can remember thinking to myself, 'My God, we've done it!'" exclaimed Major Nigel Taylor.

Yet victory came at a steep price. Over nine thousand Allied troops were killed or wounded on D-Day. The battle at Omaha alone took the lives of more than three thousand American soldiers.

The hole in Hitler's Atlantic Wall opened the way for millions more Allied forces to pour inland. The liberation of Europe could finally begin.

CHAPTER 10
Freedom at Last

Within a week of D-Day, the separate Allied troops joined together in an unbroken line across Normandy. They marched eastward toward Germany. Still, nearly a year more of fighting in Europe lay ahead.

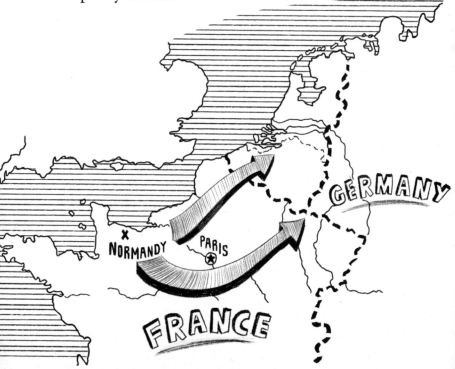

In the weeks following D-Day, the Allies landed hundreds of thousands *more* troops and supplies. In less than a month, about 180,000 tons of supplies and 50,000 vehicles were unloaded at Omaha Beach. Winston Churchill called it "the most difficult and complicated operation that has ever taken place." Just as amazing was how the ships landed. Normandy had no harbors or ports. The Allies had to make two harbors of their own and haul them to Normandy in pieces! Nothing like this had ever been done before. The makeshift harbors had about twelve miles of floating steel roadways. Breakwaters were made of giant concrete blocks, sunk into the seafloor. Each block was five stories tall and weighed more than 6,000 tons.

After three months of fighting, the Allies freed northern France. Then they marched ahead into Germany. Battle lines often formed at hedgerows, the thick banks of bushes that bordered farm fields. The Germans had dug rifle pits and machine-gun tunnels behind many of these bushes. "Fighting is from field to field and from hedgerow to hedgerow," wrote Staff Sergeant Bill Davidson, in a field report. "You rarely speak of advancing a mile in a single day. You say, instead, 'We advanced eleven fields.'" Meanwhile, Soviet troops fought their way into Germany from the east.

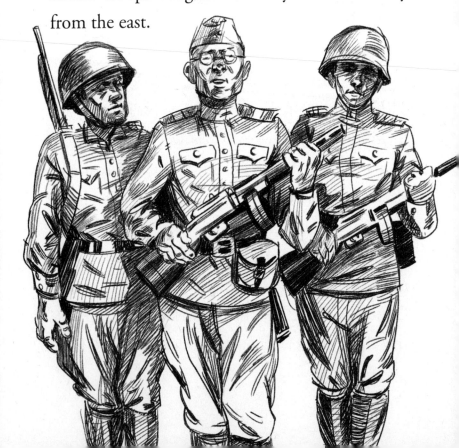

More of Hitler's horrors came to light as the troops pushed through Europe and freed millions from the Nazi death camps. The starving prisoners who had survived appeared as walking skeletons. Radio reporter Edward R. Murrow told his listeners: "I reported what I saw and heard, but only part of it. For most of it, I have no words."

Germany finally surrendered on May 7, 1945, eleven months after D-Day. Hitler had killed himself the week before rather than face defeat.

Tens of millions of people under Nazi control were now free. People around the world rejoiced. Hitler's reign of terror was over.

The war in the Pacific ended with Japan surrendering on September 2, 1945, after the United States dropped two atomic bombs on the Japanese cities of Hiroshima and Nagasaki.

World War II went down in history as the deadliest war of all time. No one knows for sure how many lives were lost. Estimates range between forty and fifty million dead.

D-Day was the turning point of World War II. On June 6, 2014, the seventieth anniversary of the invasion, United States President Barack Obama praised the soldiers: The "course of human history" hung on this "sliver of sand [at Normandy]," he said. "Our victory in [World War II] decided not just a century, but shaped the security and well-being of all posterity."

Timeline of D-Day

Aug 1943	Churchill and Roosevelt meet and set D-Day for 1944
Nov 1943	General Dwight D. Eisenhower is promoted to Supreme Commander of all Allied forces in Europe
1944	In late May, training camps empty as D-Day troops move to southern Britain
June 3, 1944	Soldiers begin boarding ships bound for Normandy
	A bad storm forces Eisenhower to call the D-Day fleet back to port
June 5, 1944 4:00 a.m.	Eisenhower gives the order for the D-Day invasion to proceed after hearing of weather break
June 6, 1944 D-Day	Just after midnight on June 6, 1944, paratroopers capture key bridges over Caen Canal and Orne river after landing on gliders
1:20 a.m.	Lieutenant Richard Winters becomes lost behind enemy lines
1:30 a.m.	Germans open fire on paratroopers over Normandy
3:00 a.m.	Shortly after 3:00 a.m., D-Day, German radar discovers the invasion fleet; enemy troops prepare for battle

Seaborne troops in the English Channel leave transport ships to board small landing boats	1:00–4:00 a.m.
Paratroopers liberate the first town in France, Sainte Mère Eglise, from the Nazis	4:30 a.m.
"Swimming tanks" are launched at Omaha; none succeed there	6:00 a.m.
The first wave of Allies lands on the beaches of Normandy, France	6:30 a.m.
British forces arrive at Gold and Sword Beaches	7:30 a.m.
Canadians land at Juno Beach; about one in two soldiers in the first wave are killed or wounded	8:00 a.m.
Allied destroyers open fire at Omaha Beach under revised orders	9:50 a.m.
German troops begin losing hold of Omaha Beach	1:30 p.m.

Timeline of World War II

1933	Nazi Adolf Hitler becomes chancellor of Germany
1939	On September 1, Germany invades Poland
	On September 3, France and Britain declare war against Germany; the Second World War begins
	On September 17, USSR invades Poland
1940	In May, German troops invade Holland, France, Belgium, and Luxembourg
	May 26–June 4, emergency boat lifts rescue British soldiers from Dunkirk, France
	In September, Japan joins the Axis powers
1941	In March, the Germans invade Africa at Egypt
	In June, German forces invade Russia
	On December 7, the Japanese bomb the US Pacific Fleet at Pearl Harbor, Hawaii
	On December 8, the United States declares war on Japan, joining the Allies
1942	On June 7, Japan loses a major battle at Midway
1943	In February, Germans surrender at Stalingrad, USSR
	In July, Allies land at Sicily; Mussolini overthrown in Italy
	In September, Italy surrenders to the Allies
1944	On June 6, D-Day, Allied troops invade Europe at Normandy
	In August, Allies liberate Paris, France
	In September, Allied troops invade Germany

On April 12, US President Franklin D. Roosevelt dies in **1945**
office; Harry S. Truman becomes president
On April 22, Russian forces invade
Berlin, Germany, from the east
On April 30, Adolf Hitler commits suicide
Germany surrenders on May 7,
ending the war in Europe
On August 6, the United States drops an
atomic bomb on Hiroshima, Japan
On August 9, the United States drops an
atomic bomb on Nagasaki, Japan
On August 15, Japan surrenders
September 2 is V-J Day (Victory over Japan);
World War II is over

Bibliography

*Books for young readers

Ambrose, Stephen E. *D-Day: June 6, 1944: The Climactic Battle of World War II*. New York: Simon & Schuster, 1997.

*Bliven, Jr., Bruce. *Invasion: The Story of D-day*. New York: Random House, 1956.

Botting, Douglas, and the editors of Time-Life Books. *The D-Day Invasion (World War II)*. Alexandria, VA: Time-Life Books, 1998.

Drez, Ronald J. *Remember D-day: The Plan, the Invasion, Survivor Stories*. Washington, DC: National Geographic Society, 2004.

Hall, Anthony. *D-Day Day by Day*. New York: Chartwell Books, Inc., 2003. Reprinted 2012.

*Miller, Terry. *D-Day: The Allies Strike Back During World War II*. New York: Scholastic, 2009.

*Panchyk, Richard. *World War II for Kids: A History with 21 Activities*. Chicago: Chicago Review Press, Inc., 2002.

Videos

American Experience: D-Day. Video. PBS. A Guggenheim
    Production Film for American Experience, WGBH Educational
    Foundation. 1994.

D-Day to Berlin. Video. BBC. 2005.

Operation Bodyguard: D-Day Deception. Video. History
    Channel. Producer/Director: Jonathan Martin. 2003.

Surviving D-Day. Video. UK, Discovery Channel. Producer: Tim
    Goodchild. Director: Richard Dale. 2010.

Websites

www.militaryhistoryonline.com/wwii/dday

www.nationalww2museum.org

The Big Three: Winston Churchill,
Franklin D. Roosevelt, and Joseph Stalin

General Dwight D. Eisenhower (center) meets with other officers

Fighter planes at dawn

US planes fly over Allied ships to the French coast

Antiaircraft fire lights up the sky

General Eisenhower speaks with paratroopers before they take off

US soldiers crowd into a landing craft

US paratrooper ready for action

Hundreds of paratroopers drop from the sky over Normandy

US soldiers exit a landing craft

US troops rush toward Omaha Beach

GI wades past German antiboat obstacles

Americans sit in the cover of their foxholes

Soldiers lift an inflatable decoy tank

Allied troops head inland from Omaha Beach

Infantry troops carefully cross a road under fire

German soldiers surrendering

German soldiers march after being captured

American soldiers rest next to rubble

World War II poster promoting
women entering the workforce

A model of Private John Steele
dangling from a church steeple

Winston Churchill speaks to soldiers who fought on D-Day

Private Frederick Hunt Kupfer, age nineteen, participated in the D-Day invasion

A D-Day memorial on present-day Utah Beach